MAN LYING ON A WALL

Man Lying on a Wall

POEMS 1972–75

by

MICHAEL LONGLEY

LONDON . VICTOR GOLLANCZ LTD . 1976

ISBN 0 575 02110 1

76-376180

ACKNOWLEDGEMENTS AND NOTES

Some of these poems have appeared previously in *Broadsheet, Caret, Encounter, Honest Ulsterman, Irish Press, Irish Times, Lines Review, Listener, London Magazine, New Humanist, New Poetry I* (Arts Council of Great Britain), *New Review, New Statesman, Penguin Modern Poets 26, Phoenix, Poetry Nation, Times Literary Supplement*; and on B.B.C. Radio 3 and Radio Telefis Eireann.

'Dreams' was published by JAMM Graphics as a poster poem with art work by John Middleton; 'Fleance' was commissioned by the Globe Theatre Trust and included in *Poems for Shakespeare 3*; twelve of the poems and four others, with cover design and frontispiece by John Middleton, were printed in a pamphlet called *Fishing in the Sky* by the Poet & Printer Press in 1975.

p.19: A *bullaun* is a square or cylindrical block of granite into which a deep hole has been cut to make a roughly shaped stone basin.

p.26: A *fleadh* is a festival of traditional Irish music, a *bodhran* a goatskin drum.

PRINTED IN GREAT BRITAIN
BY EBENEZER BAYLIS AND SON LIMITED
THE TRINITY PRESS, WORCESTER, AND LONDON

FOR BECKY, DAN AND SARAH

No insulation –
A house full of draughts,
Visitors, friends:

Its warmth escaping –
The snow on our roof
The first to melt.

CONTENTS

CHECK-UP

Let this be my check-up:
Head and ear on my chest
To number the heartbeats,
Fingertips or your eyes
Taking in the wrinkles
And folds, and your body

Weighing now my long bones,
In the palm of your hand
My testicles, future:
Because if they had to
The children would eat me—
There's no such place as home.

THE LODGER

The lodger is writing a novel.
We give him the run of the house
But he occupies my mind as well—
An attic, a lumber-room
For his typewriter, notebooks,
The slowly accumulating pages.

At the end of each four-fingered
Suffering line the angelus rings—
A hundred noons and sunsets
As we lie here whispering,
Careful not to curtail our lives
Or change the names he has given us.

THE BAT

We returned to the empty ballroom
And found a bat demented there, quite
Out of its mind, flashing round and round
Where earlier the dancers had moved.

We opened a window and shouted
To jam the signals and, so we thought,
Inspire a tangent in the tired skull,
A swerve, a saving miscalculation.

We had come to make love secretly
Without disturbance or obstacle,
And fell like shadows across the bat's
Singlemindedness, sheer insanity.

I told you of the blind snake that thrives
In total darkness by eating bats,
Of centuries measured in bat droppings,
The light bones that fall out of the air.

You called it a sky-mouse and described
Long fingers, anaesthetising teeth,
How it clung to the night by its thumbs,
And suggested that we leave it there.

Suspended between floor and ceiling
It would continue in our absence
And drop exhausted, a full stop
At the centre of the ballroom floor.

THE SWIM

The little rowing boat was full of
Friends and their intelligent children,
One of them bailing out for dear life
It seemed, while with an indolent hand

Another trailed a V on the lake
And directed it towards the island
Like an arrow. And nobody looked
As we undressed quickly and jumped in.

All of you vanished except your head:
Shoulders dissolving, and your arms too,
So opaque the element which could,
I knew, bend a stick at the elbow

Or, taking the legs from under you,
In its cat's-cradle of cross-currents
Like a bridegroom lift you bodily
Over the threshold to the island.

To risk brambles and nettles because
We wanted to make love there and then
In spite of the mud between my toes,
The weeds showing like veins on your skin,

Did seem all that remained to be done
As the creak of the rowlocks faded
And our friends left us to be alone
Or whatever they had decided.

THE GOOSE

Remember the white goose in my arms,
A present still. I plucked the long
Flight-feathers, down from the breast,
Finest fuzz from underneath the wings.

I thought of you through the operation
And covered the unmolested head,
The pink eyes that had persisted in
An expression of disappointment.

It was right to hesitate before
I punctured the skin, made incisions
And broached with my reluctant fingers
The chill of its intestines, because

Surviving there, lodged in its tract,
Nudging the bruise of the orifice
Was the last egg. I delivered it
Like clean bone, a seamless cranium.

Much else followed which, for your sake,
I bundled away, burned on the fire
With the head, the feet, the perfect wings.
The goose was ready for the oven.

I would boil the egg for your breakfast,
Conserve for weeks the delicate fats
As in the old days. In the meantime
We dismantled it, limb by limb.

RIDDLES

Soft Target

I am a soft target, head
And shoulders, a hair's breadth

Now that the lines intersect
And you nail me to the sky.

Sea-burial

We are sailors now, and grant them
—The dead men in their coffins,
The skeletons in our cupboard—

A sea-burial: our sheets
Pulled up over them, their bodies
Launched from beneath our flag.

Voice-box

An animal stirs in your throat:
To unlock that particular cage

Would be to set howling the cats
And dogs of the entire district.

Leavetakings

I jumble our souls like anagrams
Until leavetakings on the staircase,
Dressing-gowns in the cold scullery

Spell out my one apotheosis:
A foot in the door for ever, no
Belongings but what I stand up in.

Close-up

A question of connections:
Of face to face always, or

Head to head on the pillow,
These distances, a bad line.

Stretch-marks

I take on your stretch-marks,
The slack skin at belly
And breast, and would welcome

Other stigmata, wear
As blush or wide naevus
Menses, women's complaints.

Double-barrel

You solve my body like a riddle:
All of my ships in the one bottle,

A double-barrel: the answer up-
Side down at the bottom of the page.

DREAMS

1

Your face with hair
Falling over it
Was all of your mind
That I understood,

At the bottom of which
Like a windfall
I lay and waited
For your eyes to open.

2

I am a hot head
That quits the pillow,
A pair of feet
Numb with nightmare

Near the chilly lake
Of faithful swans
Or the clean mating
Of wolves in the snow.

LOVE POEM

If my nose could smell only
You and what you are about,
If my fingertips, tongue, mouth
Could trace your magnetic lines,
Your longitudes, latitudes,
If my eyes could see no more
Than dust accumulating
Under your hair, your skin's
Removals and departures,
The glacial progression
Of your fingernails, toenails,
If my ears could hear nothing
But the noise of your body's
Independent processes,
Lungs, heartbeat, intestines,
Then I would be lulled in sleep
That soothes for a lifetime
The scabby knees of boyhood,
And alters the slow descent
Of the scrotum towards death.

BELLADONNA

1

Mischievous berries release the drug
That whitens her complexion and makes
Black pools of the pupils of her eyes,

Her face reflecting my face, eyelids
A sparrow watering its wings there
Or a butterfly drowned in the cup.

2

I have surrounded her with bottles
—Whiskey, medicines, assorted drugs—
I am a drunk, an addict, and she

The genie behind the glass, released
When I drink at her mouth, when I smell
Through her nostrils these substances.

3

She and I are blood donors, prepared
As specimens for the microscope,
Transparencies of Christ's example

And, as anybody's future now,
Strangers, our identities smothered
Under the wing of the pelican.

DESERT WARFARE

Though there are distances between us
I lean across and with my finger
Pick sleep from the corners of her eyes,
Two grains of sand. Could any soldier
Conscripted to such desert warfare
Discern more accurately than I do
The manifold hazards—a high sun,
Repetitive dunes, compasses jamming,
Delirium, death—or dare with me
During the lulls in each bombardment
To address her presence, her absence?
She might be a mirage, and my long
Soliloquies part of the action.

IN MAYO

1

For her sake once again I disinter
Imagination like a brittle skull
From where the separating vertebrae
And scapulae litter a sandy wind,

As though to reach her I must circle
This burial mound, its shadow turning
Under the shadow of a seabird's wing:
A sundial for the unhallowed soul.

2

Though the townland's all ears, all eyes
To decipher our movements, she and I
Appear on the scene at the oddest times:
We follow the footprints of animals,

Then vanish into the old wives' tales
Leaving behind us landmarks to be named
After our episodes, and the mushrooms
That cluster where we happen to lie.

3

When it is time for her to fall asleep
And I touch her eyelids, may night itself,

By my rule of thumb, be no profounder
Than the grassy well among irises

Where wild duck shelter their candid eggs:
No more beguiling than a gull's feather
In whose manifold gradations of light
I clothe her now and erase the scene.

4

Dawns and dusks here should consist of
Me scooping a hollow for her hip-bone,
The stony headland a bullaun, a cup
To balance her body in like water:

Then a slow awakening to the swans
That fly home in twos, married for life,
Larks nestling beside the cattle's feet
And snipe the weight of the human soul.

WEATHER

I carry indoors
Two circles of blue sky,
Splinters of sunlight
As spring water tilts
And my buckets, heavy

Under the pressure of
Enormous atmospheres,
Two lakes and the islands
Enlarging constantly,
Tug at my shoulders, or,

With a wet sky low as
The ceiling, I shelter
Landmarks, keep track of
Animals, all the birds
In a reduced outdoors

And open my windows,
The wings of dragonflies
Hung from an alder cone,
A raindrop enclosing
Brook weed's five petals.

FLORA

A flutter of leaves
And pages open
Where, as my bookmark,
A flower is pressed,

Calyx, filament,
Anther staining
These pictures of me
In waste places

Shadowing sheep-tracks
From seacliff to dunes,
Ditches that drain
The salty marshes,

Naming the outcasts
Where petal and bud
Colour a runnel
Or sodden pasture,

Where bell and bugle,
A starry cluster
Or butterfly wing
Convey me farther

And in memory
And hands deposit
Blue periwinkles,
Meadowsweet, tansy.

POINTS OF THE COMPASS
for John Hewitt

Inscription

A stone inscribed with a cross,
The four points of the compass
Or a confluence of lines,
Crossroads and roundabout:
Someone's last milestone, propped
At an angle to the nettles,
A station that staggers still
Through tendrils of silverweed:
To understand what it says
I have cleared this area
Next to the casual arc
A thorn traces upon stone.

Clapper Bridge

One way to proceed:
Taking the water step
By step, stepping stones
With a roof over them,
A bed of standing stones,
Watery windows sunk
Into a dry-stone wall,
Porches for the water,
Some twists completing it
And these imperfections
Set, like the weather,
On the eve of mending.

Cell

After the entire structure
Has been sited thoughtfully
To straddle a mountain stream,
The ideal plan would include
A path leading from woodland,
From sorrel and watercress
To the one door, a window
Framing the salmon weir,
A hole for smoke, crevices
For beetles or saxifrage
And, for the fear of flooding,
Room enough under the floor.

Standing Stone

Where two lakes suggest petals
Of vetch or the violet,
The wings of a butterfly,
Ink blots reflecting the mind,
There, to keep them apart
As versions of each other,
To record the distances
Between islands of sunlight
And, as hub of the breezes,
To administer the scene
From its own peninsula,
A stone stands, a standing stone.

FERRY

I loop around this bollard
The beeline of cormorants,
The diver's shifts in air
And secure my idea
Of the island: rigging

Slanted across the sky,
Then a netting of sunlight
Where the thin oar splashes,
Stone steps down to the water
And a forgotten ferry.

THE KING OF THE ISLAND

The man who owns it
Calls himself the king
Of this windy island
Which is bumping now
Our starboard timbers.

These are his waters
The gannet penetrates
Without a splash, turning
On the bright sixpence
I toss there for luck.

It is like a marriage
When we ring the birds,
One fulmar especially
Whose last foothold
May have been St Kilda,

Whose heavy wingbeats
We gather from the air,
Folding flight-feathers
Along the soft body,
Protecting the eye

And brittle wrist until
We have encircled it
With a long number
The king of the island
Will read, when he returns.

FLEADH

for Brian O'Donnell

Fiddle

Stained with blood from a hare,
Then polished with beeswax
It suggests the vibration
Of diaphanous wings
Or—bow, elbow dancing—
Follows the melted spoors
Where fast heels have spun
Dewdrops in catherine-wheels.

Flute

Its ebony and silver
Mirror a living room
Where disembodied fingers
Betray to the darkness
Crevices, every knothole—
Hearth and chimney-corner
For breezes igniting
The last stick of winter.

Bodhran

We have eaten the goat:
Now his discarded horns
From some farflung midden
Call to his skin, and echo

All weathers that rattle
The windows, bang the door:
A storm contained, hailstones
Melting on this diaphragm.

Whistle

Cupped hands unfolding
A flutter of small wings
And fingers a diamond
Would be too heavy for,
Like ice that snares the feet
Of such dawn choruses
And prevents the robin
Ripening on its branch.

Pipes

One stool for the fireside
And the field, for windbag
And udder: milk and rain
Singing into a bucket
At the same angle: cries
Of water birds homing:
Ripples and undertow—
The chanter, the drones.

LANDSCAPE

Here my imagination
Tangles through a turfstack
Like skeins of sheeps' wool:
Is a bull's horn silting
With powdery seashells.

I am clothed, unclothed
By racing cloud shadows,
Or else disintegrate
Like a hillside neighbour
Erased by sea mist.

A place of dispersals
Where the wind fractures
Flight-feathers, insect wings
And rips thought to tatters
Like a fuchsia petal.

For seconds, dawn or dusk,
The sun's at an angle
To read inscriptions by:
The splay of the badger
And the otter's skidmarks

Melting into water
Where a minnow flashes:
A mouth drawn to a mouth
Digests the glass between
Me and my reflection.

'FURY'

On his mother's flank
A twist of blood, straw
Trailing to his crib
Behind the milk churns,

In the high rafters
Martins that chatter
Above his silence,
The white of his eye,

His enormous head's
Dithering acceptance
Of a breach birth,
A difficult name.

Somewhere already
The hiss of scythes,
The forking of hay
For his bony frame,

Over laid grasses
And thistles crows
Hustling to pin down
The new evictions.

I can just make out
His starry forehead
Hesitant among
Eyebright and speedwell.

TRUE STORIES
for Rebecca and Daniel

The Ring

I was ferried out to where
Petrels flung from the cliff face
Their long bodies, and underfoot
Plovers piled on pebbles
More pebbles, speckled eggs,

Four segments to each circle
Which I half-inscribed for you
By echoing both your names
And by fastening my ring
Around a fledgling's leg.

The Egg
for Daniel

It was your birth over again
Happening in my head as I let
Unfold in the palm of my hand
A tiny squeaking, a skull, feet,
Wings that the shell had compressed,

Yours the fulmar's exquisite eye
Balancing above one clean egg
And taking in all of the island,
The solitary snow goose, whiteness,
Bird lime among the sea campions.

The Nest

Next door to the tussocky well
I uncovered the lark's snug nest,
Our orderly neighbour: enough
To occupy you while you slept
Warming the eggs and silencing

The mallard's waterlogged alarum
From the bog, who, to spite the heron
And deflect a dangerous sky,
Had fouled her nest before leaving
And stained the immaculate shells.

The Wren
for Rebecca

After your two nightmares
(One about a giant bird
Lowering itself from the sky:
In the other both your eyes
Grew featureless as eggshells)

You were first to discover
A wren trapped in the kitchen:
Two pulses fluttering until
You had opened the window
On broken dreams, true stories.

HALCYON

Grandmother's plumage was death
To the few remaining grebes,
The solitary kingfisher
That haunted a riverbank.

But, then, I consider her
The last of the Pearly Queens
To walk under tall feathers—
The trophies of sweethearts

Who aimed from leafy towpaths
Pistols, silver bullets,
Or sank among bullrushes
Laying out nets of silk.

So many trigger fingers
And hands laid upon water
Should let materialise
A bird that breeds in winter,

That settles bad weather,
The winds of sickness and death—
Halcyon to the ancients
And kingfisher in those days,

Though perhaps even she knew
It was the eccentric grebe
Whose feet covered the surface,
Whose nest floated on the waves.

STILTS
for Paul Muldoon

Two grandfathers sway on stilts
Past my bedroom window.
They should be mending holes
In the Big Top, but that would be
Like putting out the stars.

The first has been a teacher
Of ballroom dancing, but now
Abandons house and home
To lift in the Grand Parade
High knees above the neighbours.

The second, a carpenter,
Comes from another town
With tools and material
To manufacture stilts
And playthings for the soul.

TRIPTYCH

Father

I have been dressed in white
So that I might absorb
Your bruises, the stubble
At your groin, the milk
Your blue veins discolour,

And supervise his birth,
Death of the afterbirth
And my own reduction to
The ghost of a terrorist
Interrogated by you.

Baby

There are hairs feathering
His forehead, lanugo,
A shadow on his limbs,
No tears when he cries
And no smile, contentment,

Convulsions, splayed toes,
Fingers separated
Beneath the quietness,
The lips that are smiling,
Breasts that weep for him.

Mother

If you could reconstruct
Two knees, the elbow
She tested water with
Or crooked like a cradle,
You would remember

Her eyes hidden behind
Colossal hands, a breast
Curved to an horizon
That soaked the sun's hair,
The features of the moon.

GRANNY

I shall give skin and bones
To my jewish granny

Who has come down to me
In the copperplate writing

Of three certificates,
A dogeared daguerreotype,

The echo of splintering
Glass when my grandfather,

In the one story he told
About her, tossed a brick

Through the parlour window
Of rowdy neighbours as she

Lay dying and Jessica
Abrahams, her twenty years

And mislaid whereabouts
Gave way to a second wife,

A terrible century,
A circle of christian names.

MASTER OF CEREMONIES

My grandfather, a natural
Master of ceremonies
('Boys! Girls! Take your partners
For the Military Two-step!')

Had thrown out his only son—
My sad retarded uncle
Who, good for nothing except
Sleepwalking to the Great War,

Was not once entrusted with
Rifle, bayonet but instead
Went over the top slowly
Behind the stretcher parties

And, as park attendant where
All hell had broken loose,
Collected littered limbs
Until his sack was heavy.

In old age my grandfather
Demoted his flesh and blood
And over the cribbage board
('Fifteen two, fifteen four,

One for his nob') would call me
Lionel. 'Sorry. My mistake.
That was my nephew. His head
Got blown off in No Man's Land.'

EDWARD THOMAS'S WAR DIARY
1 January–8 April, 1917

One night in the trenches
You dreamed you were at home
And couldn't stay to tea,
Then woke where shell holes
Filled with bloodstained water,

Where empty beer bottles
Littered the barbed wire—still
Wondering why there sang
No thrushes in all that
Hazel, ash and dogwood,

Your eye on what remained—
Light spangling through a hole
In the cathedral wall
And the little conical
Summer house among trees.

Green feathers of yarrow
Were just fledging the sods
Of your dugout when you
Skirted the danger zone
To draw panoramas,

To receive larks singing
Like a letter from home
Posted in No Man's Land
Where one frantic bat seemed
A piece of burnt paper.

MOLE

Does a mole ever get hit by a shell?
—Edward Thomas in his diary, 25.2.17

Who bothers to record
This body digested
By its own saliva
Inside the earth's mouth
And long intestine,

Or thanks it for digging
Its own grave, darkness
Growing like an eyelid
Over the eyes, hands
Swimming in the soil?

LOAMSHIRE

For years its economy has been running down
Because most of the inhabitants are poets
Who cultivate wild thyme or bog asphodel
And profess a diminishing interest in
The hidden meaning of the root vegetable.

The population explosion makes matters worse
Despite the by now famous last words of one
Who was crushed to death under his first tractor,
Or the demise of another who was kicked into
Unconsciousness for ever by a horse's hoof:

They both died smiling: and now the empty stable
That accumulates an aura of picturesque
Dilapidation, and the broken machinery
That drops petals of rust on to the relics, stand
As the shrines of a continuous pilgrimage.

Religious practice requires the sentimental
Sacrifice and complete extermination of
Such domestic animals as the pig and goat,
So that the prevalent diet has become
Badger hams, the occasional roast hedgehog,

Or, when in season, brightly coloured berries
And the unprotected eggs of rare species
Whose short memories return every springtime,
Risking naked eyes and hungry binoculars
To nest among denuded hedgerows, bare branches.

In all likelihood the number of emigrants
Would increase were it not for the sad tendency
Of the highways to dwindle to grassy byways
That meander beyond inaccurate signposts,
And the impossibility of locating,

Even if this were desirable, the county
Capital or some administrative centre
That might focus the scatter of smallholdings
And reduce the raggedly drawn boundary
To a dispute of international proportions.

MAN LYING ON A WALL
Homage to L. S. Lowry

You could draw a straight line from the heels,
Through calves, buttocks and shoulderblades
To the back of the head: pressure points
That bear the enormous weight of the sky.
Should you take away the supporting structure
The result would be a miracle or
An extremely clever conjuring trick.
As it is, the man lying on the wall
Is wearing the serious expression
Of popes and kings in their final slumber,
His deportment not dissimilar to
Their stiff, reluctant exits from this world
Above the shoulders of the multitude.

It is difficult to judge whether or not
He is sleeping or merely disinclined
To arrive punctually at the office
Or to return home in time for his tea.
He is wearing a pinstripe suit, black shoes
And a bowler hat: on the pavement
Below him, like a relic or something
He is trying to forget, his briefcase
With everybody's initials on it.

FLEANCE

I entered with a torch before me
And cast my shadow on the backcloth
Momentarily: a handful of words,
One bullet with my initials on it—
And that got stuck in a property tree.

I would have caught it between my teeth
Or, a true professional, stood still
While the two poetic murderers
Pinned my silhouette to history
In a shower of accurate daggers.

But as any illusionist might
Unfasten the big sack of darkness,
The ropes and handcuffs, and emerge
Smoking a nonchalant cigarette,
I escaped—only to lose myself.

It took me a lifetime to explore
The dusty warren beneath the stage
With its trapdoor opening on to
All that had happened above my head
Like noises-off or distant weather.

In the empty auditorium I bowed
To one preoccupied caretaker
And, without removing my make-up,
Hurried back to the digs where Banquo
Sat up late with a hole in his head.

ARS POETICA

1

Because they are somewhere in the building
I'll get in touch with them, the wife and kids—
Or I'm probably a widower by now,
Divorced and here by choice, on holiday
And paying through the nose for it: a queue
Of one outside the bathroom for ever
And no windows with a view of the sea.

2

I am writing a poem at the office desk
Or else I am forging business letters—
What I am really up to, I suspect,
Is seducing the boss's secretary
Among the ashtrays on the boardroom table
Before absconding with the petty cash box
And a one way ticket to Katmandu.

3

I go disguised as myself, my own beard
Changed by this multitude of distortions
To stage whiskers, my hair a give-away,
A cheap wig, and my face a mask only—
So that, on entering the hall of mirrors
The judge will at once award the first prize
To me and to all of my characters.

44

4

After I've flown my rickety bi-plane
Under the Arc de Triomphe and before
I perform a double back-somersault
Without the safety net and—if there's time—
Walk the high wire between two waterfalls,
I shall draw a perfect circle free-hand
And risk my life in a final gesture.

5

Someone keeps banging the side of my head
Who is well aware that it's his furore,
His fists and feet I most want to describe—
My silence to date neither invitation
Nor complaint, but a stammering attempt
Once and for all to get him down in words
And allow him to push an open door.

6

I am on general release now, having
Put myself in the shoes of all husbands,
Dissipated my substance in the parlours
Of an entire generation and annexed
To my territory gardens, allotments
And the desire—even at this late stage—
To go along with the world and his wife.

COMPANY

I imagine a day when the children
Are drawers full of soft toys, photographs
Beside the only surviving copies
Of the books that summarise my lifetime,
And I have begun to look forward to
Retirement, second childhood, except that
Love has diminished to one high room
Below which the vigilantes patrol
While I attempt to make myself heard
Above the cacophonous plumbing, and you
Who are my solitary interpreter
Can bear my company for long enough
To lipread such fictions as I believe
Will placate remote customs officials,
The border guards, or even reassure
Anxious butchers, greengrocers, tradesmen
On whom we depend for our daily bread,
The dissemination of manuscripts,
News from the outside world, simple acts
Of such unpatriotic generosity
That until death we hesitate together
On the verge of an almost total silence:

Or else we are living in the country
In a far-off townland divided by
The distances it takes to overhear
A quarrel or the sounds of love-making,
Where even impoverished households
Can afford to focus binoculars

On our tiny windows, the curtains
That wear my motionless silhouette
As I sit late beside a tilley-lamp
And try to put their district on the map
And to name the fields for them, for you
Who busy yourself about the cottage,
Its thatch letting in, the tall grasses
And the rain leaning against the half-door,
Dust on the rafters and our collection
Of curious utensils, pots and pans
The only escape from which is the twice
Daily embarrassed journey to and from
The well we have choked with alder branches
For the cattle's safety, their hoofprints
A thirsty circle in the puddles,
Watermarks under all that we say.

LAST RITES

Death-watch

I keep my own death-watch:
Mine the disembodied eye
At the hole in my head,
That blinks, watches through
Judas-hatch, fontanel:

Thus, round the clock, the last
Rites again and again:
A chipped mug, a tin plate
And no one there but myself,
My own worst enemy.

Drag-net

They can put out the drag-net:
Squads of intelligent detectives
Won't discover the hairs of my beard
Lodged like bookmarks between the pages
In even the remotest library,

Or the hairs of my head unravelling
For some Ariadne along dark
Corridors and back into my head,
Or the truth of my body, its sperm
Outnumbering the women in the world.